T0169292

CONFERENCE PROCEEDINGS

RAND

The Middle East in the Shadow of Afghanistan and Iraq

F. Stephen Larrabee

Prepared for the
Center for Middle East Public Policy
and the Geneva Centre for Security Policy

National Security Research Division

The conference proceedings described in this report were supported by RAND's Center for Middle East Public Policy and the Geneva Center for Security Policy.

ISBN: 0-8330-3446-4

The RAND conference proceedings series makes it possible to publish conference papers and discussions quickly by forgoing formal review, editing, and reformatting. Proceedings may include materials as diverse as reproductions of briefing charts, talking points, or carefully written scientific papers. Citation and quotation is permitted, but it is advisable to check with authors before citing or quoting because of the informal nature of the material.

RAND is a nonprofit institution that helps improve policy and decisionmaking through research and analysis. RAND® is a registered trademark. RAND's publications do not necessarily reflect the opinions or policies of its research sponsors.

Published 2003 by RAND
1700 Main Street, P.O. Box 2138, Santa Monica, CA 90407-2138
1200 South Hayes Street, Arlington, VA 22202-5050
201 North Craig Street, Suite 202, Pittsburgh, PA 15213-1516
RAND URL: http://www.rand.org/
To order RAND documents or to obtain additional information, contact Distribution Services: Telephone: (310) 451-7002; Fax: (310) 451-6915; Email: order@rand.org

Preface

On May 5–6, 2003, RAND's Center for Middle East Public Policy (CMEPP) and the Geneva Centre for Security Policy (GCSP) held a two-day conference in Geneva on "The Middle East in the Shadow of Afghanistan and Iraq." The conference was the fourth in a series of collaborative efforts by GCSP and RAND's CMEPP in the area of security policy.

At previous CMEPP-GCSP workshops in 1999 and 2001, participants examined, respectively, possible roles for NATO in the Middle East and the challenges to Turkey as both a European and Middle Eastern actor. The 2002 workshop, scheduled for June 23–25, 2002, was originally intended to take a broad look at issues relating to Southwest Asia, where Europe and the United States have long grappled with a range of strategic and political differences. However, in light of the terrorist attacks on the United States on September 11, 2001 and the subsequent U.S.-led military campaign in Afghanistan, the organizers decided to refocus the workshop around the specific theme of terrorism and asymmetric conflict in Southwest Asia. The workshop focused on both the global and regional aspects of the terrorist threat.

We would like to thank all of the conference participants enumerated in Appendix B.

Shahram Chubin and Jerrold Green

The Middle East in the Shadow of Afghanistan and Iraq

On May 5–6, 2003, RAND and the Geneva Centre for Security Policy (GCSP) held a two-day conference in Geneva on "The Middle East in the Shadow of Afghanistan and Iraq." The conference examined the impact of the Iraq war on the security of the Middle East and was attended by specialists from the United States, Europe, and the Middle East. This report summarizes the main issues and points of discussion at the conference.

War on Terrorism

One of the central issues at the conference was the impact of Iraq on the war on terrorism. A number of participants questioned recent optimistic assessments about al-Qaeda's demise. Al-Qaeda was, as one participant put it, "down but not out." Its capabilities and leadership had been weakened; it had not launched any major terrorist acts in 4–5 months; and Bin Laden was quiet. Nonetheless, it was too early to write al-Qaeda's obituary. Al-Qaeda had been forced to move to softer, more vulnerable targets. But al-Qaeda was still capable of inflicting pain. It had proven to be a nimble and flexible organization. While half of its leadership had been killed or captured, the other half—perhaps the most dangerous half—was still at large. Its ability to operate from Afghanistan had been severely weakened. But it was still able to operate from Pakistan. And it was still capable of replenishing its ranks.

Another reason for caution was the lack of clarity about the exact nature of al-Qaeda. While some described it as a highly centralized organization, others argued that its leadership was highly diffused. In addition, the intervention in Iraq had given al-Qaeda's struggle a new dimension: Jihad was now fused with a desire for revenge. Iraq, moreover, provided a target-rich environment. Indeed, the situation in Iraq now might be more dangerous than before the invasion because the current power vacuum and breakdown of authority made terrorist acts easier.

It was also not clear how much al-Qaeda's financial resources had actually been limited. Some of its assets had been frozen, but it was hard to know how much had not been frozen or confiscated. The loss of Afghanistan was not that much of a blow to al-Qaeda. It was still able to operate out of other areas, especially

Pakistan. And it had a vast cadre of recruits. Even if Bin Laden were dead, this would not prove to be a mortal blow because the organization was highly decentralized and not organized around one man. It was suggested that the brains of the organization were the "Egyptians" around Zawahiri.

Recent events suggest that the war on terrorism may be entering a period of transition. What we may be facing, one participant suggested, is *less organized* terrorist organizations. The emphasis appeared to be switching to *individual acts* of terrorism. The real test was whether groups like al-Qaeda still had the ability to act and were able to rejuvenate themselves.

The war in Iraq, one European participant argued, had not had a significant effect on the war on terrorism. Despite differences between the United States and Europe over Iraq, cooperation between the United States and Europe in countering terrorism remained good, she maintained. However, a new trend was emerging: Suicide bombers were now coming from Europe to Israel. Although this had been the case in earlier decades, it had not been seen in the second intifidah; and the case of the two British citizens, Omar Sharif and Asir Hanif, who carried out a suicide bombing in a nightclub in Tel Aviv at the end of April, suggested that recruitment patterns might be changing. This in turn suggested that recruits coming from Europe, a more difficult security challenge, reflected a radicalization of European Muslims. However, many participants felt that the long-term impact of the U.S. intervention in Iraq on the war on terrorism was hard to assess. Iraq probably would not have much effect on the hard-core terrorist leadership, an American participant suggested. But it could have an impact on two other areas: (1) popular support and (2) strategic support.

The impact on the popular level, he suggested, would be affected by a number of variables:

- How well the United States does in reconstructing Iraq
- How successful the Palestine-Israel "roadmap" proves to be
- How the withdrawal of U.S. forces in Saudi Arabia affects public attitudes in the Muslim world
- How political reform affects support for terrorism.

On the strategic level, state support for terrorism had diminished due to the war in Iraq. This was reflected in reduced support in Afghanistan, Iraq, Libya, and Syria. How much this will matter was not clear. But not having safe havens and camps could be important.

Several participants emphasized that the war on terrorism was a long-term struggle. There were bound to be ups and downs. Moreover, during this struggle, groups will mutate. We may not see something like al-Qaeda again. For Bin Laden, what was important was that a process had been set in motion. Other groups beside al-Qaeda would carry on the struggle.

There were already examples of such mutations. The Algerian terrorists in France, a French participant pointed out, originally saw their mission as primarily national in scope. However, this changed after they received training in Afghanistan in 1996. Thereafter, they saw themselves as international terrorists.

Participants also pointed to a close linkage between failed states and terrorism. Failed states often provided havens for terrorists. Afghanistan and Somalia provided important examples. However, the problem was not just one of failed states. A new phenomenon was emerging, one participant argued. "Failed mega-cities" were becoming havens for terrorists. Several cities in Pakistan, especially Karachi, highlighted this trend. In Pakistan, the United States had the support of the national government in the struggle against terrorism. But the national government was unable to control the cities, which had become sanctuaries for terrorist networks.

Several participants noted the difficulty of finding direct links between regimes and terrorism. There was some evidence of a link between Iraq and al-Qaeda but the evidence was tenuous and circumstantial. The Western media often stressed that 15 of the 19 terrorists who took part in the September 11 attacks were from Saudi Arabia. But, one participant suggested, this might simply have been because it was easier for Saudis to obtain a visa waiver. Thus, it made operational sense for al-Qaeda to use Saudi citizens.

Interestingly, one participant pointed out, the Palestinian issue was not initially on the al-Qaeda radar screen and was not seen as a jihadist issue, whereas Chechnya was. Palestinian groups did not want the Palestinian issue turned into an international jihad. Instead, they wanted to keep the focus on the Palestinian issue itself.

A number of participants were uncomfortable with the idea of a "war" on terrorism. They suggested that this gave the wrong connotation—that fighting terrorism was like defeating a state in a classical military sense. Defeating terrorism, they argued, required a different strategy, one that integrated political and economic as well as military means. Moreover, it was often hard to define a "win." The struggle was essentially a war of attrition. The challenge, several noted, was not to become fatigued.

4

The war could not be won, several participants argued, without addressing the underlying economic and social conditions that contributed to terrorism. They pointed to the fact that, in contrast to Asia, economic growth in the Middle East had been declining while the population in the region was growing rapidly. This would lead to a growing pool of unemployed young men who would be ripe for radicalization. Unless something was done to address these underlying structural trends, they suggested, terrorism was likely to grow.

Iraq and Iran

The conference also devoted considerable attention to the future of Iraq and Iran. The situation in Iraq, most agreed, was extremely fluid. It was thus hard to make predictions about Iraq's future at this point. Much would depend on the character of U.S. policy.

One of the key problems is the lack of a civil society. Under Saddam, society had essentially been atomized. The Baathist regime had used its oil revenues to tie large parts of the society directly to the state. As a result, society became dependent on the state. In effect, society was coopted. Those who refused to be coopted were either silenced or killed.

At the same time, a shadow state grew up that consisted of informal networks of power. The Baathist elite tried to break tribal ties and create new networks of coopted tribes and individuals. The dilemma the United States faced was: Should it try to rely on remnants of the shadow state or should it try to rebuild the state from the bottom up?

This problem was compounded, one participant pointed out, by the fact that there was no real history of party politics—as it is known in the West—in the region. Instead the region has had political movements. There was some evidence now of a return to the past—to broad political movements—which appeared to be becoming the main means of political expression. In addition, the Shi'ites were emerging as a political force in Iraq. But there was little coherence within the Shia movement in Iraq. Moreover, a Shia regime in Iraq was likely to be viewed as a competitor by Iran.

Conference participants also discussed the impact of the Iraqi war on Iran. Iran, one participant noted, had been rather satisfied with the pre-war situation in Iraq. From Iran's point of view, Iraq had been weak and contained and thus posed no serious threat to Iran. Given a choice, Iran would probably prefer a stable, weak Islamic Republic in Iraq. It wanted neither a strong Islamic regime nor a U.S. puppet. However, it feared U.S. encirclement (Iraq, Afghanistan).

Iran today faces strong political, economic, and social pressures. Its economic prospects have diminished. It faces an important youth bulge. In addition, it feels increasingly hemmed in by the U.S. presence in Iraq and Afghanistan. The problem was compounded by the fact that the United States was sending mixed messages. On one hand, the United States condemned Iran as a member of the "axis of evil." On the other, it engaged in secret discussions with Iran. But Iran was also sending mixed messages. Given these developments, there seemed little likelihood of a significant improvement in U.S.-Iranian relations in the near future.

Participants disagreed, however, on how U.S.-Iranian relations were likely to develop in the future. One school maintained that relations were unlikely to witness major improvement. A second school argued that relations were actually likely to deteriorate. Iran was a prime supporter of terrorism. This, some argued, was likely to significantly complicate U.S.-Iranian relations. The "neo-cons," it was suggested, might openly attempt to destabilize Iran. As a result, U.S.-Iranian relations were likely to get worse.

At the same time, European participants argued that there had been an evolution in European views on Iran over the last several years. As a result, U.S. and European analyses were now much closer than a few years ago. This reduced the likelihood of Iran emerging as a source of conflict in U.S.-European relations.

Iran's nuclear ambitions were also addressed. One participant argued that Iran's nuclear ambitions were unlikely to be stopped. This would have an impact on the rest of the region. However, from the Arab point of view, there was a problem if Iran was de-nuclearized and Israel was not. Other participants noted that there was also a danger that the Iranian threat might be used by some in the U.S. military to justify maintaining a large U.S. force posture, which could hinder the transformation of U.S. forces. At the same time, the U.S. presence in Iraq could be used by some Iranians to justify stepping up the Iranian nuclear program.

Syria and the Levant

Syria proved to be one of the big losers in the Iraq crisis. The Syrian government miscalculated. The Syrian leadership had thought that the war would last longer and was caught off guard by the rapid collapse of the Saddam regime. Moreover, the leadership initially failed to appreciate the depth of the political earthquake precipitated by Iraq's collapse. The fear of U.S. sanctions, however, makes it likely that Syria will cooperate with the United States and put pressure on Hezbollah and the Palestinians. The Syrian leadership also is likely to take a more flexible attitude toward the "roadmap," and might even be brought into resuming negotiations directly itself.

The collapse of Saddam's regime has had two important effects. First, it has shifted the balance of the power in the region. A new Iraq—possibly a Shi'ite Iraq—will emerge. Moreover, U.S. forces are now in the heartland of the Middle East. Iraq's removal also disturbs the balance in the Northern Tier.

Second, Iraq's collapse has launched a new inter-Arab debate. It has made it harder, one participant argued, for Arabs to associate themselves with democracy because democracy has now become associated with U.S. intervention in Arab eyes. At the same time, it has stirred great resentment in the Arab world. One outcome could be that the Syrians speed up their WMD program. They will also want to protect their presence in Lebanon.

Several participants questioned why Syria was so slow to react. Why didn't the leadership appreciate the depth of the likely changes? Why didn't the old guard associated with Assad's father see what was coming? The older Assad had been quite good at sitting out crises. This time, the regime egged on the resistance and apparently could not foresee the easy U.S. military victory. So what went wrong this time?

Several factors, it was suggested, helped explain why the Syrians were caught off guard and were slow to react.

- First, Syria faced a more assertive U.S. leadership.
- Second, Syria found itself in a less favorable economic situation.
- Third, the regional situation is much different today.

Bashar Assad's inexperience also played a role. Foreign policy had not been his top priority. He initially concentrated on domestic reform and created expectations that proved difficult to fulfill.

Some participants suggested that the U.S. intervention in Iraq would increase the salience of the Palestinian issue. This depended, others argued, on how the process of reconstruction in Iraq plays out. If the United States gets bogged down in Iraq, Washington will have less time and inclination to pay attention to the Palestinian issue.

Much will also depend on Israeli policy. Sharon, one U.S. participant argued, does not believe in withdrawing from the Golan Heights. He believes that the peace process will weaken Israel by attrition—step-by-step. However, Sharon might, the participant argued, be willing to accept a Palestinian state and the evacuation of the settlements as an interim solution. However, Prime Minister Abbas had to deal with Hamas before Sharon would move. The roadmap, he asserted, was a "guide," a starting point. It was not cast in concrete and not likely to be the ultimate solution.

Turkey and Jordan

Conference participants also examined the implications of the war in Iraq for Turkey and Jordan. The strong electoral victory of the Justice and Development Party (AK) in November 2002 (34 percent of the popular vote) had prompted expectations that the gridlock in Turkish policy in the last few years would be broken. Due to the peculiarities of the Turkish electoral system, the AK's 34 percent of the vote gave the party a majority in parliament (365 seats out of 550). Moreover, many of the other mainstream parties had failed to cross the 10 percent threshold needed to obtain representation in parliament. Thus, for the first time in many years, Turkey had a strong government that faced little opposition.

However, since then, many of the early hopes that the AK might bring about positive change had dissipated and the party was now in disarray. The Iraq crisis proved to be a critical test that the party was ill-prepared to meet. The Grand National Assembly's refusal to authorize the deployment of U.S. troops on Turkish soil to open a second front through Northern Iraq had seriously weakened the party.

There were several reasons the government resolution failed. One was the strong opposition to the war among the Turkish public. Nearly 95 percent of the public was opposed to the war. Moreover, there was a strong feeling among the Turkish population and elite that Turkey had not been adequately compensated for its sacrifices in the 1991 Gulf War and that the United States had reneged on its promises made at that time. Several former U.S. officials, however, disputed that the United States had made such promises.

A second key factor was the inexperience of the AK leadership. It was one thing to run a city like Istanbul; quite another to run the Turkish government. Third, Turkey overestimated its strategic leverage. Many members of the AK thought that the United States could not prosecute the war against Iraq without the use of Turkish territory. They felt that Turkey was in a strong bargaining position and could hold out to achieve its goals. Eventually, the United States would be forced to accept Turkish terms. This proved to be a major strategic miscalculation.

An intriguing question was why the Turkish military had not lobbied harder for passage of the resolution authorizing the deployment of U.S. troops on Turkish soil, especially since the military regarded security matters as their prerogative. Two explanations were put forward: (1) the military hung back out of deference to EU demands that the military take a lower profile in Turkish politics (2) the military wanted to embarrass the AK and see it "stew in its own juices."

The second proposition, many felt, was closer to the mark. But, one participant noted, all sides appear to have miscalculated. Given the AK's strong majority in parliament, few had expected the vote would fail. The military had wanted to have it both ways. They wanted to force the AK to take responsibility for the controversial decision, which would be unpopular, especially with its own rank and file. At the same time, they expected that the resolution would be approved, since the AK had such a strong majority in parliament. They were thus caught off guard when the resolution failed.

Fortunately, the war was short and the United States suffered few casualties. As a result, several participants stressed, the repercussions on Turkish-U.S. relations were not likely to be too serious or long-lasting. Relations had been hurt but not irrevocably so. Although the specialness of the relationship had evaporated, the United States was unlikely to seriously downgrade relations with Ankara. Some participants argued that the outcome had actually been beneficial. The United States, they suggested, was far better off than if the Turks had intervened in Northern Iraq. This could have seriously complicated the post-conflict prospects for stability in Northern Iraq.

Turkey also was better off, one participant maintained, as a result of the outcome of the conflict. The idea of a strategic partnership, he suggested, had been overblown and had created expectations that could not be fulfilled. Now the United States and Turkey could develop a normal relationship.

This might be true, another argued, but the situation looked very different from Ankara. Relations with the United States had been damaged, perhaps not irrevocably, but damaged nonetheless. Turkey's leverage in Northern Iraq was diminished as a result of the negative vote in parliament. The AK had been weakened and Turkey had lost much needed economic assistance that could have helped it to buffer the impact of the current economic crisis. Cyprus had also, in part, been a casualty of the Iraq crisis. As a result, Turkey's chances of opening accession negotiations with the EU had been set back.

The impact of the war in Iraq on Jordan was also discussed. Jordan, it was noted, had taken a different stance in the recent Iraq crisis than it had in the 1991 Gulf War. In 1991, it had sat on the sidelines. This time the United States had made very clear that Saddam would be removed. Thus Jordan had to look after its own security interests. It had quietly permitted the U.S. military to use its airspace, deploy Patriot missiles on its territory, and station about 3000 troops, including some Special Forces, there.

Jordan, a Jordanian participant noted, wants to see a pluralistic, democratic Iraq. It also has a strong stake in the "roadmap." It was unclear, however, whether the roadmap would be successful. Jordan's economic relations with Iraq, however, were likely to change. Under Saddam, political calculations had driven relations. The historic relationship between Iraq and Jordan had given Jordan an economic edge. Before the war, Iraq provided Jordan with about 100,000 barrels of oil a day, half at discount prices and half free. The Jordanians sold the oil at a markup, which added about $200 million a year to its budget. Moreover, Jordan paid for the oil not with cash but with Jordanian products worth about $300 million a year. However, under the new regime in Baghdad, Jordan was unlikely to enjoy the same privileged status that it enjoyed under Saddam. Market considerations would drive relations, not political calculations. Local business will have to take advantage of the new economic conditions, but so far they have been slow to do so. The United States is expected to help out economically this time.

The Arabian Peninsula

The discussion of the impact of the Iraq war on the Arabian Peninsula centered around two broad issues. The first was the impact on the regional balance of power, particularly Saudi Arabia's role. While it was difficult to say exactly what the impact of the Iraq war would be on the Arabian peninsula, several participants suggested that it could lead to shifts in the regional balance of power. In particular, the balance of power in the GCC could shift away from Saudi Arabia. Qatar, they noted, was emerging as a major player in the Gulf. It wanted to get out from under Saudi domination and had clearly thrown in its lot with the United States. Qatar's policy and regional ambitions were of concern to Saudi Arabia, but its ambitions were not congruent with Qatar's size and real possibilities. Qatar, some participants suggested, seemed to be "punching above its weight."

Iraq's evolution, several participants stressed, could have an important impact on the Gulf States. If Iraq becomes a pro-U.S. democracy, this could have a liberalizing impact on the Gulf monarchies. The U.S. victory would end an era in which Gulf States lived under an Iraqi threat. At the same time, there was a possibility that Iraq might be integrated into a Gulf security system. In such a case, a new Iraqi-led bloc could emerge as a counterbalance to Iran, but also to Saudi Arabia's detriment.

Saudi Arabia was likely to be affected as well. A reassessment of U.S.-Saudi relations was already visible before the outbreak of the war with Iraq. But it was likely to gain greater momentum as a result of the war. The Saudis, one participant pointed out, had actually been more helpful in the Iraq war than many observers had expected. Publicly, they had been rather critical of the war, but behind the scenes they had rendered considerable support to the United States. In any event, the war was likely to result in a lower U.S. military profile in Saudi Arabia, which in turn could help reduce tensions in U.S.-Saudi relations. Saudi Arabia would remain sensitive to continued turmoil in Iraq, it was noted.

Iraq oil, participants agreed, could have an important impact. Once Iraq's oil came back on line, this could reduce Western dependence on Saudi oil. But it was stressed that it would take time for Iraq to increase its oil production and that with the best will in the world, Iraq could not replace Saudi Arabia's vital role as "swing producer" in the event of crises and shortfalls; for that, it would need the unused spare capacity of two million barrels a day that was a uniquely Saudi asset. Nonetheless, either a strong pro-American and reformist Iraq or a weak, unstable Iraq could lead to greater social unrest in Saudi Arabia, several participants warned. One important consideration will be the nature of the regime that emerges in post-Saddam Iraq. If a Shia-dominated republic should emerge in Iraq, Saudi Arabia would feel threatened. In such a case, Riyadh could move to intensify relations with Pakistan and might look to Islamabad for nuclear reassurance.

Iranian nuclear ambitions are another important factor that will affect the regional balance. If Iran develops nuclear weapons, the United States, one participant suggested, might be prompted to provide a nuclear umbrella to the Gulf States. However, this would only work, another noted, as long as Iran did not have nuclear weapons that could reach the United States. Once Iran achieved the capability to deliver nuclear weapons that could hit the United States, the calculation would change.

A second dominant theme during discussions was the prospects for internal reform in the region, especially in Saudi Arabia. Several participants noted that there was pressure for reform both from the top and from the bottom. Both Bahrain and Qatar had recently taken steps toward greater political liberalization. An amorphous movement for reform had also gained strength in Saudi Arabia since the 9/11 attacks on the World Trade Center and the Pentagon.

However, the parameters of reform are not clear. Most of the leaders in the region were interested in some form of "decompression"—that is, a relaxation of some restrictions—not genuine liberalization. This was designed to buy time and postpone major reform. However, the Iranian experience called into question whether slow, selective reform could work.

In Saudi Arabia, the problem is compounded by the fact that Saudi Arabia faces an important succession issue. Prince Abdullah is nearly 80. His most likely successor, Defense Minister Sultan, is nearly 79. This succession is likely to have an impact not only on Saudi Arabian politics but on regional politics as well. However, despite these pressures for change, most participants felt that the Saudi regime would not collapse and would be able to continue to muddle through, although with diminished influence.

The Impact on Transatlantic Relations

The final session was devoted to transatlantic relations. Most participants agreed that the Iraq crisis had badly damaged transatlantic relations, especially Franco-U.S. relations. The crisis had been badly handled on both sides and it would be difficult to pick up the pieces. As far as Iraq's future was concerned, it was unclear what role Europe would—or would be allowed to—play. At the moment, one European suggested, the United States seemed intent on prolonging the divisions that had emerged during the Iraqi crisis and playing one part of Europe off against the other. But over the longer run, he felt the United States would return to a more traditional policy based more firmly on cooperation.

Another participant argued that there were deeper structural problems. These problems have been exacerbated by the technological gap between U.S. and European forces. This gap was growing and there was no prospect that it would be reduced. With the exception of the British, no European forces have the capability to project and sustain forces in areas where the United States is likely to be engaged militarily. The problems existed not just with America's European allies. This was even more true with regard to friends and partners in the Gulf and Middle East. The Saudi Air force was the only air force in the region with which the United States could cooperate. These differences were reinforced by important economic and demographic trends that could exacerbate the social and economic instability in the region. Reconstruction of Iraq was likely to have little impact on these broader trends.

The United States is undoubtedly in a league by itself militarily, a European participant conceded. It doesn't need Europe militarily. However, Europeans, he argued, look at the problem differently. They don't believe military power alone can solve all problems. They still want to maintain a Western community that includes the United States. However, he acknowledged that considerable damage had been done to Franco-American relations and this damage was unlikely to be undone quickly or easily.

Several Americans argued that the United States had hoped Europe would develop into a true political and military partner. In these hopes, however, the United States had been disappointed. Europe had not become the partner that America had hoped it would become, particularly in the military field.

One American argued that an effort to develop a partnership in the Middle East might actually make things worse. Earlier attempts to involve the Europeans in Middle East, he said, had complicated matters because the Europeans sought to outbid the United States with the Arabs. Only when the Europeans were willing to build a relationship of trust with Israel would such a partnership be able to work. Europe, he argued, needed to make clear that it was willing to be sympathetic on issues that really mattered to Israel if it wished to play a significant political role in the Middle East.

Differences also emerged between U.S. and European participants regarding the "Barcelona process." The United States, one American claimed, had been consciously excluded from the Barcelona process. European participants countered, however, that the Mediterranean, especially North Africa, was in Europe's backyard. Europe had its own interests in the region and it was only natural that it developed its own dialogue to address these problems. The Barcelona process was designed not to exclude Americans but to complement U.S. peace efforts in the region.

On the peace process and roadmap and especially U.S. willingness to get involved even-handedly, on the question of the response to Iran's nuclear ambitions, and on reconstruction in Iraq as well as on the revival of the Atlantic alliance, there will be opportunities for coordinating policies and repairing relations in coming months, but none of these issues is resolved and each will be better tackled jointly.

Appendix
A. Programme

Sunday, 04 May 2003

19h30   *Dinner at the Hôtel d'Angleterre*

Welcome:
Ambassador Gérard STOUDMANN, Director, GCSP

Keynote address: *Iraq and After*

Dr. Martin INDYK, Senior Fellow, Foreign Policy Studies,
Brookings Institution, Washington, D.C.

Monday, 05 May 2003

09h00–09h15   **Welcome and Introduction**

Dr. Shahram CHUBIN, Director of Research, GCSP

Dr. Jerrold D. GREEN, Director of International Programs
and Development; Director, Center for Middle East
Public Policy, RAND

09h15–10h45   **War, Political Unrest, and Terrorism**

Chair: Dr. Shahram CHUBIN, Director of Research,
GCSP

Terrorism Trends and Potentialities: An Assessment

Dr. Bruce Hoffman, Director, RAND Washington Office

Discussants: Mrs. Thérèse Delpech, Directeur chargé
de la Prospective, CEA, Paris

Dr. David GOMPERT,
Emeritus Vice President, RAND

10h45–11h15	*Coffee Break*
11h15–12h00	**General Discussion**
12h00–13h00	*Buffet lunch*

13h00–15h00   **Repercussions on Iraq and Iran**

Chair: Dr. Jerrold D. GREEN, Director of International Programs and Development; Director, Center for Middle East Public Policy, RAND

Repercussions on Iraq

Dr. Toby DODGE, Research Fellow, Economic and Social Research Council, Centre for the Study of Globalisation and Regionalisation, University of Warwick

Discussant: Mr. Hussein AGHA, Analyst

Repercussions in Iran

Dr. Shahram CHUBIN, Director of Research, GCSP

Dr. Jerrold D. GREEN, Director of International Programs and Development; Director Center for Middle East Public Policy, RAND

15h00–16h00   **Repercussions on the Levant**

Chair: Dr. James A. THOMSON, President and CEO, RAND

Presentation

Dr. Volker PERTHES, Stiftung Wissenschaft und Politik (SWP), Berlin, Germany

Discussants: Dr. Ahmad KHALIDI, Senior Associate Member, St. Antony's College, Oxford University

Dr. Martin INDYK, Senior Fellow, Foreign Policy Studies, Brookings Institution, Washington, D.C.

16h00–16h30	*Coffee Break*
16h30–17h30	**General Discussion**
19h30	*Dinner at "Chez Jacky"*

Dinner speech: *National Interests as a Guide to U.S. Behaviour*

Dr. James A. THOMSON, President and CEO, RAND

Tuesday, 06 May 2003

09h00–10h30   **Repercussions on Turkey and Jordan**

Chair: Dr. F. Stephen LARRABEE, RAND Corporate Chair in European Security and Senior Staff Member

Dr. Philip J. ROBINS, Lecturer in the Politics of the Middle East, St. Antony's College, University of Oxford

Gen. Ali SHUKRI, St. Antony's College, University of Oxford

10h30–11h00   *Coffee Break*

11h00–12h30   **Repercussions on the Arabian Peninsula**

Chair: Dr. Martin INDYK, Senior Fellow, Foreign Policy Studies, Brookings Institution, Washington, D.C.

Presentation

Dr. Joshua TEITELBAUM, Research Fellow, Moshe Dayan Center for Middle Eastern and African Studies, Tel Aviv University

Discussant: Dr. Ibrahim KARAWAN, Director, Middle East Center, University of Utah

12h30–13h30   *Lunch*

13h30–15h00   **Impact on Transatlantic Ties**

Dr. Anthony H. CORDESMAN, Arleigh A. Burke Chair in Strategy, Middle East Studies Program, Center for Strategic and International Studies, Washington, D.C.

Mr. Gilles ANDRÉANI, Associate Professor, Université Paris II Panthéon-Assas, Paris

15h00–15h30   **Concluding Session: The U.S., Europe, and the Middle East**

Dr. Shahram CHUBIN, Director of Research, GCSP

Dr. Jerrold D. GREEN, Director of International Programs and Development; Director, Center for Middle East Public Policy, RAND

18h00   **Public Talk: War and Peace in the Middle East: Where Next for U.S. Policy?**

Dr. Martin INDYK, Senior Fellow, Foreign Policy Studies, Brookings Institution, Washington, D.C.

20h00   *Dinner*

B. List of Participants

Mr. Hussein AGHA, Analyst

Mr. Gilles ANDRÉANI, Associate Professor, Université Paris II Panthéon-Assas, Paris

Dr. Shahram CHUBIN, Director of Research, GCSP

Dr. Anthony H. CORDESMAN, Arleigh A. Burke Chair in Strategy, Middle East Studies Program, Center for Strategic and International Studies, Washington, D.C.

Mrs. Thérèse DELPECH, Directeur chargé de la Prospective, CEA, Paris

Dr. Toby DODGE, Research Fellow, Economic and Social Research Council, Centre for the Study of Globalisation and Regionalisation, University of Warwick

Dr. David GOMPERT, Emeritus Vice President, RAND

Dr. Jerrold D. GREEN, Director of International Programs and Development; Director, Center for Middle East Public Policy, RAND

Dr. Bruce HOFFMAN, Director, RAND Washington Office

Dr. Martin INDYK, Senior Fellow, Foreign Policy Studies, Brookings Institution, Washington, D.C.

Dr. Ibrahim KARAWAN, Director, Middle East Center, University of Utah

Dr. Ahmad KHALIDI, Senior Associate Member, St. Antony's College, Oxford University

Dr. F. Stephen LARRABEE, RAND Corporate Chair in European Security and Senior Staff Member

Dr. Robert LITWAK, Director, International Studies Division, Woodrow Wilson International Center for Scholars, Washington, D.C.

Dr. Volker PERTHES, Stiftung Wissenschaft und Politik (SWP), Berlin, Germany

Dr. Philip J. ROBINS, Lecturer in the Politics of the Middle East, St. Antony's College, University of Oxford

Gen. Ali SHUKRI, St. Antony's College, University of Oxford

Dr. Paul B. STARES, Director of Research and Studies Program, United States Institute of Peace, Washington, D.C.

Dr. Joshua TEITELBAUM, Research Fellow, Moshe Dayan Center for Middle Eastern and African Studies, Tel Aviv University

Dr. James A. THOMSON, President and CEO, RAND